AF413390

concordant chaos

Poems Written by Kayla DiStefano

Bronzepit Publishing

ISBN: 979-8-218-39165-2

DEDICATION

This book is dedicated to my parents, my sister, my partner, and my children.

Thank you for supporting me and helping me make my dream come true.

TABLE OF CONTENTS

SLEEP

Lying in bed you think, "Life is tough."
Your best just isn't good enough.
You say you're prepared, they call your bluff, it's time to go back to sleep.
Ruffling the covers you hear a sound, like a giant weight just hit the ground.
You look down and what you found, you were dreaming, go back to sleep.
Rain is trickling from the sky. The wispy clouds are rolling by.
Mascara on your pillow as you start to cry, the worst way to fall asleep.
Crackling thunder shakes your bed. You grasp your sheets and throw them over your head. And right now you wish you were dead.
It's just a storm, go back to sleep.
Open one eye, not left but right, your phone keeps flashing extremely bright.
You pick it up and put it out of sight. Come on just go to sleep.
Your alarm goes off and you start to whine. You can't pretend that you are fine.
Want to complain? Get in line, you're not the only one who couldn't sleep.
The day begins gloomy and slow. Put on a smile so they don't know.
Sometimes you must just let it go.
Maybe tonight you'll get some sleep.

COFFEE

For goodness' sake I'm not awake.
 I need to get out of bed.
Though I want to stay,
 I should start my day and get some knowledge in my head.
 I need one drink so that I can think and keep me from falling asleep.
 It gives me control- and warms my soul and where I buy it is cheap.
Started to drink it when I was young trying not to turn burn my tongue.
 It stunts your growth, that explains a lot.
 I can drink a whole pot, with milk or cream, without it I'll scream.
Hot or iced, latte or pumpkin spice.
The varieties never seem to end.
It's like a nice hug and it is my drug, that's why coffee is my best friend.

SWEET TOOTH

It comes in a little heart shaped box,
either a circle or a square.
What's inside?
Take a bite, do it if you dare.
Some are filled with coconut, others buttercream.
The ones that melt inside your mouth make your taste buds scream.
 Peanut butter, caramel, even cherry filled.
On a rollercoaster ride of flavor but just one you're not fulfilled.
Some can crunch, some can spread and some you can even drink.
Some that taste like tangerine, and some that are colored pink.
It takes you to a euphoric place where you feel relaxed and free.
One more piece will do no harm but save a piece for me.

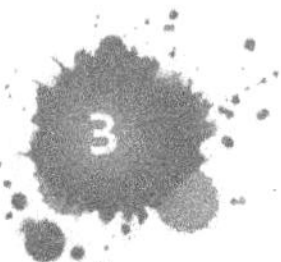

THE BOY WHO LIVED

Out by yourself or with your friends
 From school everyone knows who you are.
They recognize your face, dark brown hair, glasses, and scar.
Even though you talk to snakes you are one of the good guys.
Unlike the cowardly blonde-haired boy who sat back and just told lies.
For everything you went through you weren't on the journey alone.
Remembering back to where it all began with the Sorcerer's Stone.
You don't pick the wand; the wand picks you. That's what you were told.
You defeated the basilisk saving the girl making you incredibly bold.
Expecto patronym is what you'd say when you were under attack,
but who is the mysterious one who saved you and Serius Black?
You were entered in a tournament trying hard to not get maimed.
Ending up in a cemetery with he who must not be named.
Your scar hurt, you touched your head when he looked at you, you'd wince.
You used his spell and found out that he was the half-blood prince.
"I'm going to keep going until I succeed or die."
Considered a hero but don't close the book yet, this is not goodbye.

ONE TRUE LOVE

You can't use it as a weapon, but you can use it as a drug.
You use it when your thoughts run wild, and you need to unplug.
It fills you up when you're empty and will leave you satisfied.
It will make you forget about all those times, you cried.
It brings back all the memories, the good ones and the bad.
You blast it when you don't want to listen to your mom and dad.
It pleases and relaxes you and changes the way you feel.
It gives you the sense of being in charge and the cards are yours to deal.
It gives you strength and boosts you up like you can take on the world with ease.
 Life is hard to unlock, but music, will lead you to the keys.

HIM

You always thought they'd be hard to find because your past
clouded up your mind.
You never thought that love was all hearts and roses,
but another door opens when the last one closes.
The overwhelming feeling of being swept off your feet,
 by the person of your dreams, you never thought you'd meet.
The dates, the conversations, and the endless grins,
This is where a new life begins.
Time is spent in each other's embrace, in his or her arms is
the safest place.
The way you can sit and stare into their eyes,
you know that they are life's greatest prize.
 How it feels to walk with your fingers intertwined,
you think of your future and leave your past behind.
From the one person that you care for and admire, a soft kiss
on the lips sets your body on fire.
The ring on your finger means you're in it for the long haul,
 they're the love of your life and you found them after all.

FEELING

Spinning like a ceiling fan,
my thoughts are running wild.
Chest is tight, anxiety is high, can't stop feeling riled
Up in things I can't explain, wish you could journey inside my
brain.
A mess of words and blurry pics,
hours of songs, tears, and tricks.
I chew my nails and bite my lip, constantly thinking about
jumping ship.
Got shaky legs and sweaty hands, trying not to cancel plans.
Spinning like a ceiling fan, my thoughts are running wild.
Wanting to remember, the last time that I smiled.

WINTER

Silky sheets under my skin. Windows open, letting the record spin.

A candle is lit, aroma fills the air.

The flame is dancing, nothing can compare.

What's left on is a single sock, pillows on the floor and the door unlocked.

It feels as if time has stopped.

Those racing thoughts inside my head have dropped down underground where I hope they'll stay,

bringing in the blue skies instead of grey.

Falling asleep with a braid in my hair, a smile on my face and one foot bare.

The flame goes out as the wind comes in, it's time to let the new year begin.

PUG

Walking into the store, why you're there you're not sure,
but when you saw him, the answer was there.
Those big round eyes made your heart triple in size.
You squealed and made everyone stare.
He was short and round and made a wheezing sound,
oh, so cute you could not deny, he was little and young, with a long pink tongue,
 you knew that he was your guy.
 Touching his short dark hair, you thought, "he's the one for me."
He jumped in your lap and started to nap, and you were overcome with glee.
When you got back, you gave him a snack and a big hug.
You named him Dan and he was your man.
You got yourself a pug.

SMILE

Close your eyes and free your mind and breathe in deep, my dear.
 The whispers are inside your head, but there's no need to fear.
 Break away from the insanity that spins your world around.
Escape from all your darkest days and burn them to the ground.
Don't think that because you've fallen, you can't get on your feet.
Stand back up with bloody knees and face the problems that you meet.
You'll encounter misery, unhappiness, and strife.
Nobody said anything was easy, that's why they call it life.
Move forward with your dreams and make it all worthwhile.
Don't let anything get you down because you deserve to smile.

TEN YEARS

Where will you be ten years from now?

Will you be in a city full of rushing cars in a place with the one you love?

Will you be in the country in the open-air gazing at the stars above?

Will you have the job of your dreams the one you'll keep til the day you die?

Will you be out in the street begging for food struggling as the weeks go by?

Will you make something of yourself and try to prove that the others were wrong?

Will you fall and not get up and show they were right all along?

Will you strive to justify, you can make it through the day without a tear?

Will you let your anxiety overcome you, making your path unclear?

Will you do what's best for you and not let anyone get in the way?

Will you continue to be yourself with every passing day?

Where will you be ten years from now? A question that will make you think.

Don't think too hard or too long because life will pass in a blink.

ANOTHER DAY

Another day, another dollar.
Another day, another chore.
Another day, another fight.
Another day, another bore.
Another day, another heartbreak.
Another day, another time.
Another day, another teardrop.
Another day, another crime.
Another day, another mistake.
Another day, another pain.
Another day another job.
Another day, another strain.
Another day, another flaw.
Another day another ache.
Another day, another pill.
Another day, another break.
Another day, another hour.
Another day, another breath.
Another day, another doubt.
Another day, another death.

DREAM

In a room full of people, filled to each wall, you're stuck in the middle of it all.
The feeling of being invisible is one felt way too often.
The worst part is you would rather be stuck in a coffin.
Trying to scream but nothing will come out.
Your eyes fill with emptiness, sorrow, and doubt.
Suddenly, the room fades to black, the people are gone,
there's no turning back. You're the only one there, as you
really were before, hopes were high,
you deserve so much more.
You feel alone, like you were at the start,
it feels like your world is falling apart.
Take out the blade and feel the blood fall,
it's a way of forgetting it all.
Jolted awake by your loud clock alarm.
It was only a dream but look at your arm.

BELIEVE

Reach for the dope. Trying to cope.
No reason to mope. Do not lose hope.
Life can be grand. Just take a stand there's room to expand,
just take my hand!
 No need to be blue, there's plenty to do.
Just start anew and show what you can do.
Do not ask why, just focus, and try. Wipe your tears, don't cry.
Let your creativity fly. It's hard to admit that you wanted
to quit,
just one little slit, that would have been it.
You didn't leave, so roll down your sleeve.
 Those goals you'll achieve if you just believe.

R N R

How beautiful your melody,
 the sound that you devise.
You carry a beat so carefully; I knew it was no surprise.
Sing, strum, or beat the drum, whichever one you choose.
 It's simple enough for everyone, like learning to tie your shoes.
The lights on your face, while you're up on stage, make you feel like a star.
One, two, three, four, five, six strings on your guitar.
Hands are shaking walking up to the mic, you are about to go on.
You open your mouth and start to sing the lyrics that you've drawn.
Break out of your shell, dance, and wiggle to the sound,
You fly so high with music in your veins, you never touch the ground.
You let it become who you are, you're not afraid to lose control.
It's what you live for, it's all you know.
You were born to rock and roll.

CEST LA VIE

Go out? Stay in? where do we begin?
Trying to catch the demons buried in the skin.
Breathe in then flick, there goes the cancer stick.
Unraveling the lies that have spread so quick.
Oh, what a shame, love burned like a flame.
Melted like a candle because it was all a game.
Scratches on the knees, ears buzzing like bees,
a heart just sinks and starts to freeze.
Life's a bitch, can't get out of the ditch,
The frozen mangled heart can't take one more stitch.
Out of tune, and like a typhoon going crazy like a wolf howling
at the moon.
Eyes are now closed, starting to doze, falling limp like the
petals of a lifeless rose.
Too much to bear, couldn't be saved by prayer.
 Everything is silent, except one last breath of air.

ONE MORE DAY

She sits alone with her hands on her knees, her back to the world, her eyes on the trees. Her stringy hair falls across her face, with her unlaced shoes in this miserable place.

She takes the time to roll up her sleeve, what she's done to herself she cannot believe. Her stomach is empty and growling in pain.

She thinks of the weight she doesn't want to gain.

Her makeup-less face is pale and rough; she thinks she's not good enough.

She wants to but can't get her life on track.

She never looks forward; she always looks back.

Her shattered heart is too mangled to mend.

She thinks that this might be the end, but she gets up and walks away saying "I guess I can handle just one more day."

MAKE IT STOP

Scratching at the ground trying to escape the hell you've come to know.

Bloody fingernails dig into the earth and shiny tears fall in a row.

Mouth stapled shut so the flood of words you can't speak won't spill out.

A permanent frown lies on your face from all the years of trouble and doubt.

Scrapes and bruises cover your flesh from your head down to your feet.

Ears blown out from all the lies, screaming and deceit.

Cover up with makeup to hide the pain shown on your face.

Feeling lost and empty and in need of a warm embrace.

The ground starts to crumble, and you let yourself fall.

Nobody will save you in this town after all

Pointing, teasing, tricking, and laughing, you thought they were your friends.

They only act like they care now as your wounded body descends.

Your eyes shoot open with chills on your skin, why is it so bright.

It was a nightmare, the moon shines in, lay back down, sleep tight.

TRYING

Trying your best but it's hard to stay strong.
Holding back tears when they ask you, "what's wrong?"
You want to be the protector, so nobody gets hurt,
but no matter what you do you get kicked in the dirt.
Weighing you down your shoulders carry too much.
You dream of relief and your lover's sweet touch.
Sleepless nights worried and afraid.
You're exhausted and drained and starting to fade.
Anxiety through the roof, your hands starting to shake.
You don't ask for much, you just need a break.
Not directly involved but it still affects you.
Always pushed in the background, though you manage to pull through.
Tired of feeling hopeless and lost in the crowd.
Not craving attention just someone to be proud.
They all come first because of how much you care.
Just searching for a moment to get a breath of fresh air.
You keep pushing forward, happy is what you will be.
Sometimes it's hard but c'est la vie.

STRONG

Let me be now, can't you see that I'm the one in misery.

Set me free you'll be rid of me. You'll no longer have to hear my plea.

 In the shadows all these years battling my demons and my fears.

Hiding when I burst into tears, reemerging when the tension clears.

I shut down from all the fights, the sleepless nights seeing the morning lights.

Stepping outside with holes in my tights, shivering as the brisk air bites.

Wishing that it's just a dream. Wanting to stand up and scream.

With the same reoccurring theme, things just went to the extreme.

Trying to be the one that's strong so we can move along and sing another song.

With everything that has gone wrong I know that it won't be lifelong.

I really have no right to moan I'm aware that I am not alone.

Although my heart is not made of stone, I have grown a solid backbone.

HOW IT STARTED

Pencil to paper, pencil to mouth.

Thoughts in my head but the words won't come out.

Scribble a note, then erase it real quick. It's on the tip of my tongue but the line won't stick.

 Incorporate a simile, use the words "like or as".

That's what my teacher told me every poem has.

I write to express myself when I'm not feeling so hot.

What helps is a little coffee, okay maybe a lot.

Inspiration is everywhere I just must look.

Writing down what I think in this crumpled notebook.

Getting the hang of this now but I won't keep you all day.

Time to take the pencil off the paper and put it away.

FRIENDS?

You're not the person you used to be, the friend that I once knew.

The person who would stand up for me, the one that I could turn to.

What happened to the friendship, that blossomed into something strong?

It crumbled into ashes when infatuation came along.

Dropped in the dust is how I felt as you slowly drifted away,

to the temptation that was lust; and your heart being led astray.

I said I'd always be there for you and that will never change, but the person you have come to be, to me, is simply strange.

They say that people come and go and that one thing I knew, but what leaves me speechless to this day is that, that person was you.

LIVE

Your muscles are tense, you bite your lip, your head throbbing in your hands.
Sweating uncontrollably being drowned by life's demands.
How do people live this way, they sleep, they work, they die?
What you think is great, is mediocre to them, so why do you even try.
It's plain to see that you're unhinged but you're not the only one.
Sad to say, you thought about staring down the barrel of a gun.
What you get and what you deserve are completely different things.
Yet you take whatever life throws at you waiting to see what tomorrow brings.
You tell yourself that happiness isn't something you can buy.
It's something you must create on the days you want to cry.
Even though you don't have everything, you find it in your heart to give.
 Be determined you can push through your struggle.
You only have one life, so live.

I AM

I am the calm before the storm, but the monster under your bed.

I am the little joke that makes you laugh, but I'm the pounding in your head.

I am the sweet frosting on a birthday cake but the aching in your tooth.

I am the friend that will hold your hand but will tell you the bitter truth.

I am the sun that will make you smile but will burn your sensitive skin.

I am the luxurious comfy bed but I'm the walls that come caving in.

I am the harmonious melody, but I can sometimes skip a beat.

I am the extravagant fresh new car but I'm the pothole in the street.

I am the new house that you've dreamed of but I'm the paint chipping off the door.

I'm the new tattoo that you loved so much but I'm the blood dripping on the floor.

I am the shoe that fits just right but I'm the blisters on your feet.

I am the deep breath that you breathe in, but I am your last heartbeat.

NOTHING NEW

Lost and alone, I know the feeling.

Pain in your head staring at the ceiling.

Shaking and weak, too tired to stand.

You must get up they won't hold your hand.

Others have it worse and you know it's true.

Life is tough but you'll make it through.

Find something to smile about and lift your head high.

Break out of your box and be less shy.

Stop the arguing you're not always right.

Just talk to them, there's no need to fight.

Try new things how bad could they be, you must be a little more carefree.

Change is coming and it will be snappy.

Don't say "what if" just do it, you'll be happy.

THAT NIGHT

As the water cascades out of the sky, I sit by myself and wonder why.
It was supposed to be a night of fun, but it turned into three against one.
How stupid of me to think you were a friend.
But now I am stuck trying to defend myself against people I've never met, and this is something I could never forget.
Things like this happen more than they should, but the ones who are punished, are those who've done good.
 Surrounding myself with the ones that care, and soon my story will be easy to share.
As for now I ask for my friends to support me til this rough patch ends.
Gonna light this cancer stick and take a deep breath in.
Everyone has their scars, but not all are on their skin.

WRONG THINKING

Trapped in a box, with stitches on my mouth and I cannot say a word.

Fighting the tears each passing day I know it sounds absurd.

I try to have hope, but I'm just shot down I don't know what to think.

I thought you cared but I was wrong, you ripped my heart out and let it sink.

I can't do this again it wears me out, I just need to get away.

I wish you could see what this does to me, but you just turn your head the other way.

I don't want to be involved and yet it always sucks me in.

I thought I knew what was best for you, but I guess I'll never win.

I want to get into my car and just drive til the gas is gone.

Or disappear with the one I love so I have a shoulder to cry on.

Tired of this mess that keeps bubbling up I just want it to be done.

Until that day, I'll be stuck in this box ripping the stitches out one by one.

IN HIS ARMS

Staring at your face in the mirror trying to fake a smile.
It's the only thing that you can do, you've been doing it for a while.
Thinking about his cracked dry fist coming at you like a wrecking ball.
Your body is a punching bag, and he feels no shame at all.
A crystal tear falls down your face like a leaf falls off a tree.
You thought love was cozy and warm but in his arms aren't where you want to be.
He's a dog barking orders at you every night and day, when he puts his hands on you, you think he's going to pay.
He pushes you down and you try to get up, but you're a bug being stomped to the ground. Afraid that he may finally end it and your body will never be found.
Your brain starts to speak, as you grow weak you just want to flee. You thought love was cozy and warm but in his arms aren't where you want to be. You see the lights; his hands are cuffed it's finally going to end.
A tiny smile grows on your face you no longer need to pretend.
Behind bars now he's doing his time you are finally free.
You thought love was cozy and warm and in his arms you will no longer be.

RAIN

Heart is racing with every breath you take, thinking that this was your last mistake.

The clock stops ticking as your body grows weak, lips are numb, and you can no longer speak.

The scrapes on your knees tell a detailed story, depriving you of happiness and glory.

Just relax, it will be over soon; all your hopes are lying strewn.

The rain pours down, heavy on the street.

The steam rises, from the insufferable heat.

The sky is grey with no sign of the sun, no glimmer of hope, you've come undone.

Your eyes go black with a blank faced stare.

Turning blue from the lack of air.

Your head hits the ground with an emphatic boom, it's over now, you're in your tomb. The thick red blood puddles around your frame, they said that you were the one to blame. Your skull is broken but you feel no pain, left out to bleed in the pouring rain.

FIX

I can't keep up with all this racket.
It feels like I am in a strait jacket.
Bouncing around this padded room.
Trapped inside just like a tomb.
Screaming, crying blood shot eyes.
I feel like a boat about to capsize.
The meds are coursing through my veins.
 Can't take too much or I'll be locked in chains.
Shiver, shake and a little cold sweat.
This is the punishment that I get.
Thought I could quit the little bag of tricks.
So much for that, nice quick fix.

LIFE

Life is strange, dig a little deeper.
We're flies on walls, waiting for the reaper.
Clouds roll by as we age each day.
The world spins slow as our bodies decay.
Try to suppress things with a drink, a pill or two so you don't have to think.
Think about the pain and hurt you've felt, or all the cards that you've been dealt.
Life is strange, but we don't ask why, we are living just to die.

WAITING

Sitting and thinking and making up things, I cannot get out of my head.

Not happy, not sad, confused, or mad, just wish I had more tears to shed.

I am so confined inside my mind I'm driving myself insane.

Wanting to shout but the words won't come out, it is so hard to explain.

Biting my lip til the skin falls off, cracked and ready to bleed.

Not sure about my next step, wish my thoughts weren't so hard to read.

A lump in my throat, a fluttering heart, my mouth is so fucking dry.

Day turns to night; night turns to day and all I see is grey sky.

It too shall pass, is what they say.

Good things will come just hang tight.

So, for now I'll wait with sweaty palms for the end of the tunnel light.

DRINK UP

The ice melts into the poison that runs through her veins.
She tries to stop but she's locked in chains.
The taste on her lips makes her thirsty for more.
Another sip turns into two, three and four.
Stuck in her mind now the voices are real.
She tips her head back so she's unable to feel.
Her vision is blurred, and she starts to stand, but she can't
leave the room without the drink in her hand.
She fills up the tub for a relaxing soak, trying to forget that
her life is a joke.
The faucet runs on as water cascades to the floor.
Blacked out now from that last pour.
 Blood starts to pool with nowhere to drain, the tiles turn
red, she no longer feels pain.
She can't move and she can no longer think.
She had no clue that she'd had her last drink.

MASK

There is only so much that a smile can hide,
worn like a mask to keep true feelings inside.
Feet dragging, back aching, and constant puffy eyes.
Faking a laugh while withholding small cries.
The sun may be shining, but a dark cloud lurks.
Don't give yourself away, you do whatever works.
In moments of loneliness you think, "why me?"
A great show you put on so eloquently.
They're counting on you so just play pretend.
Just take a deep breath is what they recommend.
Sleep deprived, belly growling, seems like there's no end in sight.
Keep that mask on a little longer, and you will be alright.

AGE

The once smooth and supple skin now cracked and wasting away.

The prior sparkling green eyes are shielded by glasses to this day.

The bright smile from ear to ear turned straight into a frown.

From fashionable clothes and dazzling shoes to a drab blue hospital gown.

A singing voice that made people turn, now a whisper, that's hard to hear.

Once blessed with luscious brunette locks, grow grey with each passing year.

A fireball of energy now sits with hardly a spark.

Trying to remember better days but the mind is in the dark.

They say with age comes wisdom, that's the story I've been told, but there's a lot of things that are left unsaid about us getting old.

GOOD-BYE

Craving the kiss, craving the touch, and the whispers in the dark.
 And of course, I'll miss the "slap" on the wrist because it always left a mark.
Nothing beats being wrapped in the sheets embraced by the one you "love."
Nothing is more bleak than a tear on your cheek and all the feelings you must shove, down into the hollow pit of your chest so empty and longing for light.
Trapped inside a crowded mind counting every sleepless night.
Boiled up, to the point of no return, with glass shattered all over the floor.
Can't sweep this one under the rug, you can't do this anymore.
A clenched fist turns to an open palm, knuckles bloodied and raw.
The silence speaks volumes, time to go.
That is the last straw.

ROUGH

Open the bottle, pop another pill.
Putting down the razer with another void to fill.
Mascara on the pillow, broken glass is on the floor.
Skip another meal, ribs protrude a little more.
Head is pounding hard, getting tough to take a breath.
Starting to come to terms, with the thought of death.
Pulling up the covers and starting to drift away.
The world will keep on spinning, it's just another day.

THE END